December 2004

Dear Sadie,

This past year and a half has been a very rough road for me to travel. My journey has been hard. Through it all I have discovered the greatest gift of all - friends such as yourself. I will value you as a friend always and keep it close to my heart forever. May God Bless you this Holiday Season and throughout all your years to come. Always remember Sadie the true gifts from our Lord.

Merry Christmas Sadie
Love
Sandy Rogers

THE
JOURNEY

BY
SANDY ROGERS

TATE PUBLISHING, LLC

Published in the United States of America
By TATE PUBLISHING, LLC
All rights reserved.
Do not duplicate without permission.

All Scripture references are King James Version,
unless otherwise indicated.

Book Design by TATE PUBLISHING, LLC.

Printed in the United States of America by
TATE PUBLISHING, LLC
127 East Trade Center Terrace
Mustang, OK 73064
(888) 361-9473

Publisher's Cataloging in Publication

Rogers, Sandy

The Journey / Sandy Rogers

Originally published in Mustang,OK:TATE PUBLISHING:2004

1. Death, Suffering & Consolation 2. Recovery

ISBN 1-9331484-7-0 $10.95

Copyright 2004

First Printing: December 2004

DEDICATION

In Memory of my beloved husband
HAYWARD GEORGE ROGERS, JR
June 29, 1950 - March 26, 2003

This book is also a special tribute
to my daughters,
CHRISTINE AND TAMMY,
who stood by me every step of the way
and never stopped believing in me.
My daughters have never stopped loving
me through all of this, and I will be forever
grateful for their love.

Love,
Mom
July 2004

TABLE OF CONTENTS

FOREWORD

This book is for you who might think you are not normal. It deals with the many feelings you "will" experience after the death of your loved one. My husband and I were married for 31 years, 6 months and 14 days when he died. The loss of my husband has left a hole in my heart that no matter what I do cannot be filled. Whether you have been married for a day or a lifetime, losing a loved one is a traumatic, life-changing event. No words or actions can take the pain away. These are my feelings, words, and emotions in this book. I hope it will help you to know that you are completely normal. May God bless whoever is reading this book. Know that God will be your only strength and salvation. He will lift you up on angels' wings. He will cry with you; but most of all, He will be there in your darkest hour. He will lead you and direct your life. Thank Him everyday for all of your blessings and know that He loves you and holds you and sustains you in your every waking hour. This is a story about my "Journey" through the healing process. I hope it will give anyone who is reading this comfort in knowing that when they say time heals, the words are true. May God Bless and Keep You Always.

CHAPTER 1

THE DIAGNOSIS

I remember I was getting ready for work one morning and looking at my husband; I noticed his skin looked awfully yellow to me. He told me he had not been feeling well for a couple of weeks and had started having diarrhea. I told Hayward over and over again, he needed to see a doctor. He said the diarrhea was just nerves. The diarrhea actually lasted a couple of years, now that I look back on it.

When I look back on it now, I can clearly see all of the telltale signs of cancer: long naps, no appetite, no energy, and fatigue–constant fatigue. I would get so angry at him for coming home from work and just sitting in the chair, watching television and going to sleep.

I remember very well saying, "You have been home for over an hour. Why couldn't you have started dinner and helped out a little around here?"

He would always say, "I'm sorry, you're right, Honey. I should help more. I'm just so tired."

All the time he was tired. I wish every day I could take back those words. Words, words, words, we hurt each other so much with unkind words. I know that every relationship has its ups and downs, but I look back now and wish with all of my heart I could take back some of those words, another part of normal life. Good grief, we were married for over 31 years. Of course there are going to be good times and bad times. What we need to realize is it is perfectly normal to fight and to have rocky spots in your marriage.

Anyway, getting back, soon he was having trouble eating without getting sick. He would walk the floor for hours, trying to make his stomach feel better. Tums, Prilosec, Previcid, nothing seemed to be working. For anyone who knew my husband, eating was his favorite pastime. That was the great thing about him; he really enjoyed food, any food. Holidays were his all time favorite. I remember family gatherings; I would get so mad at him. He would pile his plate so high, and I would be so embarrassed. What I wouldn't give to be embarrassed now. The thing of it is no matter how much he ate, he never gained weight. As a matter of fact, I would be envious of that. I just look at chocolate and gain five pounds. I am sure we have all felt that way. But, unfortunately, in the end the one thing he loved the most was taken away from him completely.

He finally made his trip to the doctor's office, thank goodness. They thought it was only an ulcer. An ulcer you can live with. He was scheduled for a CT scan of his stomach. I'll never forget that day. They found some questionable things in his abdomen, kidneys and intestines, but they just weren't sure of its exact nature. Next an endoscopy was performed. I remember the doctor calling me in to look at the results. Mrs. Rogers, we have found a very rare tumor in your husband's intestines.

To tell you the truth, it really didn't sink in. I thought, *well, just take it out*. They couldn't even biopsy it because it was so hard; they couldn't break through the shell. I guess I was just very naive. I have always been one that held a positive attitude that everything can be fixed. If you can't fix it, then I will. It didn't turn out that way.

Then we had the review with the doctor. By the way, that doctor, I won't mention his name, is very kind, and I still think of him often these days. He came to our house when my husband was in his hospital bed in our living room a week before he died, and told him he was the bravest person he'd ever had the good fortune to meet. Those words ring in my ears day and night. My husband was indeed a very brave man up to the very minute of his passing. I miss him every day of my life.

The diagnosis was very unclear, "We just aren't sure we'll need to do surgery, biggest mistake of all. Everyone knows, if cancer is involved, cancer tissue cannot heal." My husband at this point was so positive, he figured he'd have the surgery and then he would eat healthy and the cancer would be cured, just like that. So going forth, that is what was in his mind. A month before his surgery, he was on clear liquids and baby food. Even the baby food was too much for him to take. He would still walk the floors in so much pain.

Unfortunately, that is not how it turned out. The day before my husband's surgery, he sat me down and said we needed to talk about what would happen if he died. I just did not want to hear that; I wouldn't even talk about it. I did not want to say those words out loud. He told me he wished to be cremated, but if I really needed to have a place to visit, I could have him buried, which is what I did. I don't know if that was right or wrong. But I do go to the cemetery every now and then and talk with him and sometimes get mad at him and sometimes I even kick his stone. I know that sounds cold, but that is my way of dealing with all of the pain. I don't have anywhere else to vent.

Some will think that maybe I didn't honor his wishes, but when you're gone you're gone. His spirit was gone, and just the shell of a very sick man remained. It really doesn't matter what happens to the body. Finally, he is at peace and resting in the best place possible. Heaven. Although my husband wasn't a very religious man, he had a very strong relationship with our Lord. My husband would give the shirt off his back to anyone. And he gave of himself continually to anyone in need. He was never judgmental or critical of anyone, he just accepted people for who they were. A trait that I wish I had. God has taken away his pain and mine still remains. Doesn't seem fair does it?

I can still remember the day of the surgery. I think we both knew what the outcome would be; I just really didn't want to face it. I wish to this very day that he didn't have the surgery. It was completely downhill from there. I really feel he would have lived just a little bit longer. But I can honestly say his quality of life would have probably been worse, and he probably would have suffered even longer. I would never have wished that for him. And for anyone who may say I'm wrong in this, remember, these are my thoughts, and none of us know what God has planned for us. God certainly doesn't want us to suffer, and He cries right along with us.

I was sitting outside in my garage when two birds came into my garage and sat there looking at me. In my heart I knew he was going to die. I didn't want him to have the surgery; I really felt that he was going to die that day. I even knew the time; it was going to be 1:37 P.M. When my husband died, the time on his death certificate was 21:37 P.M. The two, I believe, represented the two birds.

My husband didn't die that day. I remember sitting in the waiting room while he was in surgery with my pastor, my daughter and my brother, just looking at the clock every minute and just waiting for 1:37 to come and to be called by the doctor. When the doctor did finally come out and talk with us, it was very bad news. The cancer had spread all throughout his intestines, and he also had a large mass in his abdomen and over his kidneys. He said the prognosis is very grim. I really do not remember too much from that point on, it was pretty much a blur. He had Spindle Cell Carcinomatosis, a very rare cancer. The tumor could not be removed and it was causing 85% blockage in his intestines. No solid food could pass through. Therefore, a bypass was performed from his stomach to another part of his intestines.

It is of my family's opinion that when the surgeon opened him up, he should have seen that it was hopeless and closed him back up. But all doctors fight with hope against all odds and do their best to try to cure the patient. After surgery, my husband had a tube coming out of his abdomen for the overflow from his stomach.

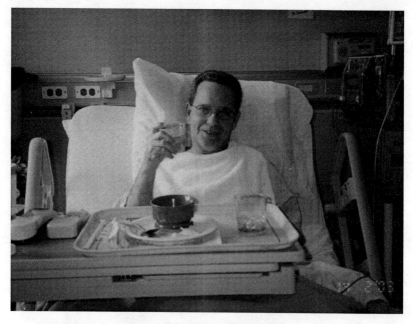

Hayward Rogers, March 2003
This picture was taken a week after his first surgery. Even baby food
and liquids were very hard for him to get down. We were cheering
him on because he was able to "drink" everything on his tray.

As he lay there in his hospital bed with the orange
Jell-O going straight into the tube, I would actually get mad at
him for allowing that to happen. Why, why, why won't you let
that food go into your body for nourishment? Please forgive me
for such thoughts. Okay, it's time to get out of bed and get some
exercise so you'll become stronger. God Bless him, he did it. He
did it over and over again, but he wasn't getting any stronger,
he was just getting weaker and weaker. I felt so hopeless and
helpless. Why did God allow this to happen? What did I ever
do wrong to deserve such punishment? It wasn't fair! All the
time thinking of myself! It was my husband who was suffering,

my pain was emotional. I stayed with him every night in that hospital. My family would get very angry at me; they wanted me to go home and get some rest. How dare they ask me such a thing? He needed me. When I went home, it was just to take a shower and put on some clean clothes; then I went right back to the hospital.

My brother finally stepped in and made me go home. He stayed with my husband at the hospital, but I didn't get any sleep because my thoughts were with my husband: Is he taking care of him? Is he helping him sit up in the bed? Is he getting him a drink? It went on and on. That is the only night I went home.

About day 5 at the hospital, he started to develop excruciating pain in his back. We all thought it was from lying in the bed too long. One particular night, he was in so much pain and I couldn't stand to be so helpless. I couldn't bear his pain. I actually went down into the hospital chapel and prayed that God take him. I didn't want him to suffer like this. God didn't take him that night.

He had now developed an abscess. His colon wasn't communicating with his intestines anymore; therefore, there was no outlet for his waste. He had to endure another surgery and another tube. Now two bags had to be emptied and monitored hourly. As it turned out, my husband endured three surgeries during his last two months of life.

Finally, on the 10th day of my husband's hospital stay, I decided we were going home, and I didn't care what the doctors said. I packed up his whole room, flowers, cards, books, everything. Of course the doctor did not let us go home that day. Two days later though, he said we could try it.

We went home on Friday. We went back to the hospital on Monday. His kidneys started to fail. He couldn't keep any liquids down. Another surgery was performed, and he received a central tube for feeding because he couldn't tolerate the stomach tube feeding anymore. Now it was TPN (Total Parenteral Nutrition) in the central tube, empty two bags, check his blood sugar, and give an insulin shot if his sugar gets too high. Now I also had to learn how to deal with the fact that he was going to die, there were no ifs, ands, or buts about it. It was just a matter of time.

I stayed up around the clock, and watched my husband die. I remember the doctor signing the do not resuscitate order thinking, *How can you be so cold? How can you give him no hope?* He just lay there and accepted his fate, which he had already accepted anyway. The surgeon told my husband he couldn't predict how long he had, but he estimated four months at the longest. In reality he had 10 more days.

Hospice began coming in. God Bless that organization and one nurse in particular who took care of him. She was so kind and so caring. I happened to see her at a hospice breakfast that our company sponsored just a little while ago. She was wonderful to him, to me, and to my whole family. I thank God everyday for her and their organization. Everyone shared with me that I was not to let them into my home because they were just there to "help" him die. So very untrue! They were there by my side every step of the way.

CHAPTER 2

THE REALITY

I remember vividly the second trip to the hospital. I didn't stay this time. My mother came down to comfort me and be with me for moral support. I believe it was his second day in the hospital, and he announced that he was going to die.

"How can you say such a thing?" I said. "How do you know that?"

He stated in very matter of fact manner, "God has told me I am going to die."

"Why?" I asked him.

He said, "I have accomplished everything on earth that I was meant to do." He could accept it; however, I could not.

I do remember driving home at 4:00 A.M. to take a shower and change my clothes. I thought, *what a relief, he is going to die.* This thought was followed by, *how could you think such a thing as this; how can you be relieved?* I can't explain it, but such a peace came over me. I knew in my heart his words were true. Now, if I could only figure out a way to deal with all of this.

Finally, his suffering and mine would be over. He had been in the hospital for a week the second time that arrangements were made for hospice to come in. I was so scared.

Family came, and everyone had ideas on how they could

make him better–Give him special food, which he couldn't keep down anyway. Give him special supplements, which had to be ground and put in any liquid he could get down. Any liquid that went down usually came back up anyway. Vomiting was a new way of life. Everyone was hoping against all odds. I would scream inside, *please just leave him alone and enjoy what time he has left on earth.*

Pray, that'll do it. We'll just pray away your sickness. It's your fault that you're not getting any better; you are not asking God to heal you. Read the Bible. Take communion. Have a positive attitude. People just didn't understand, but he did. We were the ones that were sick, sick with hope we could cure him. After all, we knew everything.

The Bible tells us in Matthew 7:8 " . . . *ask and you shall receive. . . .*" If you don't believe, it's not going to happen. I remember being so angry at everyone. I also remember saying to them, "When God has decided it's your time, there is nothing you can do about it. He makes the rules not us."

They would argue with me, "It's his fault; he has to believe it."

My husband was smarter than all of them. He did believe. He had the clues, not us. My husband was at peace with his new found information. We were not. He was very brave. He just smiled and went along with everything, never argued or said leave me alone. He knew it was our pain that was in the way.

Sleep, sleep oh precious sleep. I got very little of it then. I would sometimes get so angry at him when he called in the middle of the night. I wasn't a nurse and my nerves were stretched to the max. No one could care for him but me, so I thought. I wouldn't allow anyone else to take care of him. They just wouldn't do it right. I remember the day that I finally broke. It was a Sunday, and his abscess was no longer draining correctly into his bag. In other words, it was all over his body, and I honestly thought his intestines were coming out. I completely lost it. I started screaming and crying and carrying on, saying I just couldn't do this anymore. My family was there trying to console me. I had reached my breaking point. I had been doing this for two months now: monitoring the liquids in the bags, cleaning tubes, making meals, bathing him and trying to take care of myself. I had reached the end. He whispered in my ear, "It's alright, Honey; I am going to help you."

I looked at him in shock, "What do you mean you're going to help?"

He just nodded his head in silence. I knew then, it was the beginning of the end. He was going to die, and I finally had to face it.

At that point my oldest daughter took over and got him cleaned up. All the while my family was telling me, this was bound to happen because I didn't let anyone help before this point. I was the only one who could take care of him.

The very next day upon waking after 2–3 hours of sleep with much shame from the day before, I knew it was time to make funeral arrangements.

I called the funeral home on Monday, March 24, 2003; my brother went with me to make all of the arrangements. For some reason, I just knew this was going to be the week that I would lose my husband. I even planned for the calling hours to be held on Friday and the funeral for Saturday. I just went through the motions at that time and just planned for the inevitable of what was going to happen that week. On Wednesday, March 26, 2003, at 9:37 which reverts to 21:37 PM my husband died. I had now lost my best friend and the love of my life.

CHAPTER 3

THE FINAL DAYS

How do you tell someone goodbye? Hayward and I were high school sweethearts. I can't ever remember a time without him. I had such a crush on him when we were in junior high school, but he was not interested in me then.

It wasn't until we were freshmen in high school that he showed any interest in me. I remember the first note he ever wrote to me. It went like this: *When I get some wheels, would you go out with me?* Oh, I was so happy when he wrote me that note. I went home after school that day and showed everyone in my family and called all my girlfriends; I was so happy.

I can remember our first date. We were going to go to the movie *The Bible,* but we didn't make it to the theater because we got into a car accident. We never saw the movie. It was our seventh date before he finally kissed me goodnight. I was starting to think it a little odd that he didn't kiss me before then.

When I did finally get my first kiss from him, that was it; I was totally in love. Later, I asked him why he waited so long. He said he was afraid of me. He knew that I was the marrying kind. After the first kiss, it was very easy for him to kiss again. This thought still makes me smile.

We married when I was 19 and he was 21. He was a 20 year Air Force Veteran, and had fought in the Viet Nam War. The doctors told us the type of cancer he had was a direct result of his exposure to Agent Orange. I have been fighting the Veterans Administration since his death (actually before his death).

right: Our Wedding Day
August 12, 1971
Eating the wedding cake

left: Our Wedding Day
August 12, 1971
Getting ready to leave
for our honeymoon

We married and lived the Air Force life. My first trip away from home was to Germany, where both of our daughters were born. We had such fun in those days, and we met lots of good friends, some of which I still keep in contact with to this day.

Next we were stationed in Michigan, then on to the Philippines, Arizona, and finally New York. When we retired, we moved to North Carolina. Our home was Massachusetts.

I can't tell you the many things we battled and faced in those years. We all think we are going to have the perfect life. I don't know if there is any such thing. We had many good years together, and for that I am very thankful. We had two beautiful daughters whom I cherish above all else. They have become two very beautiful women. One is very stubborn and strong like her mother and the other is very kind, caring, and sometimes very insecure like her father. Nonetheless, they have been the joy of my life.

They both grew up with a mother they regarded as the matriarch of the family. Neither of them ever wanted to do anything to disappoint me. I was always the decision maker, disciplinarian, and role model. You name it, I was it to them. Yet, when faced with life's very cruel twist, all of these things were now null and void. So I thought anyway, at the time.

It's hard to say what feelings you should have when faced with your loved ones oncoming death. I tried to be so strong during all of this that I never took the time to grieve. I had to be strong for him, strong for my daughters, and strong for our families.

Since I had to care for him and everyone else, who "the heck" was going to take care of me? I felt that I didn't need anyone. I could do it alone. Everyone was wrong, I was the only one who knew what to do and what to feel. Of course, I was headed for disaster.

I was so tired during those last two months; I honestly don't know how I made it through. God was beside me every step of the way. I didn't see it then though. I just went through the motions, day after day, never allowing myself to feel or think. If I had allowed my thoughts and feelings to take over at the time, I don't think I would have made it through.

My only thought was *I had to get him home and out of the hospital.* I wanted him to be surrounded by the people and things he loved. I wanted him to die at home, so he wouldn't be in some cold hospital room with doctors and nurses around. He needed to be with those he loved. During that time everyone would say, "He (God) never gives you more than you can handle." The response I felt was: *how dare they use that phrase; they have no idea how I'm feeling or hard it has been on me.* I was tired and irritable all the time. I felt that no one cared about me. I was very selfish, I guess. In reality, when I look back on it, I was not selfish at all, just very vulnerable.

I had no release for my pain. I just had to see him through to his death. "I" had to be the one to take care of him. After all, he was my husband; no one knew him better than I did. I wasn't going to share that with anyone. I couldn't feel my daughter's pain because I was too involved in my own pain. Now, that I look back on it, if I had shared caring for him, maybe they would have felt like they had a part in it.

My oldest daughter came and lived with us for Pete's sake, so I wouldn't be alone and she could help. My youngest daughter lived in Washington state and has three young children, and so it was impossible for her to come home. She wanted to come though, very desperately. But I never allowed anyone to help. I could do it all.

I watched him day and night getting sicker and sicker, thinner, and weaker. I would actually get angry at him. Why can't you get any better? Why are you allowing yourself to die? Why are you not fighting to stay alive and watch your grandchildren grow? Why are you not fighting to stay alive and be with me? Why, why, why? There were so many unanswered questions. You were so positive up until this point, why aren't you continuing to fight. I can't bear the thought of not having you with me. I can't do it alone.

The last week of my husband's life was emotionally draining for all. His parents, sister and niece came down from Massachusetts to visit him. His father, very weak from a bad heart, had to bring oxygen tanks with him because he had such breathing problems. Bless his heart, it meant the world to my husband to have his family there. His youngest brother and wife also came down from Massachusetts. It was very hard on everyone to see their older brother and son in that condition. He was in a semi-coma and really didn't know most of the time what was going on. It was almost like he was disassociating himself from all of us. I didn't know if he was asleep or awake. He never closed his eyes once during his final days. I don't know if he was too scared or if his body was shutting down and didn't know how to close his eyes. I remember the last few days; I would lie in his bed with him and just hold on to him. By doing this, I thought surely he will know how much I love him and he will have the strength to go on. I believed I could will him to live.

As I spent my time bathing him, reading to him, and monitoring the fluids, I realized that the fluids weren't adding up. They are changing; they are not clear anymore. The abscess and the stomach fluids were now the same. Something was wrong, very wrong. He could no longer get out of bed. I remember distinctly the last night he was able to get out of bed to go to the bathroom. We were on our way into the bathroom when all of a sudden he became very disoriented and thought he was in Vietnam. He started falling, and I was panic-stricken! I called my daughter and she was able to help me to get him into the bathroom where I could get him seated. That was the end of his walking. From that point on, it was a urinal, then eventually adult diapers.

Vietnam, 1969
Hayward was 19 years old when this picture
was taken. Quite the looker, isn't he?

I thank God that he didn't know what was going on because he would have felt that he had lost his dignity. I would never have wished that for him. I can remember how embarrassed my daughters were when they had to help me at this point. I couldn't lift his body by myself to put his diapers on. Their father was always their Rock of Gibraltar, and they couldn't stand seeing their father in this condition. Their hearts were broken, but we got through, day by day and minute by minute.

I would lie in bed with him and tell him continually it was all right to go. I would be alright I would say to him over and over again. My oldest daughter could not bring herself to do this. She would get very angry at me for doing so. I believe she had the hardest time of all. She couldn't let go. She didn't understand why he couldn't be healed. God said we only need to ask and it will be given. She still has some issues with God. She blamed the doctors, God, and everyone else who tried to help. She did not want to lose her father. She is the one that still hurts today. Unfortunately, she has many of my traits. She has now taken on the role of mother, matriarch, decision maker, etc.

She and I often butt heads. When I look back on it now, I know the reason my husband couldn't let go. He knew there was a lot of tension between us and he wouldn't go until we had made peace with each other–until he knew that we would be all right. During his last couple of days, he was awake long enough to give everyone a message except for me. His words to me were, "Your message will come. You will know when the time is right." I still have not figured out what that meant.

Some of the things that happened before his death were really odd. God was right there with us the entire time, and we just couldn't see it. The time had come that I had to make the call to our youngest daughter; it was time for her to come home to say goodbye. My brother went to the airport to pick her up. Not a word was said from Raleigh to New Bern. When she finally arrived, he woke up and announced to all that he had been given one more day to spend with his daughter. He kept looking at his watch and asking what time it was. I believe he knew the very hour and minute he was going to pass because in the end, that is all he had left. Our youngest arrived on Tuesday, on Wednesday he died.

He was quite happy on Tuesday during the times that

he was lucid; he was sitting up in bed and clapping his hands to the Christian music we were playing. Wednesday, everything changed. He did not wake at all. His heart was beating so fast, we could actually see it through his chest.

The nurse told us that he had a very strong will to live; his heart was the only working organ in his body at that time. It was beating at 250 beats per minute.

I remember every detail of the moment of his death. My daughters and I were sitting on the couch surrounding his hospital bed, talking about when my husband and I were dating. It was silly, talking about the type of car he drove, our favorite music, and the things we used to do for fun. We never shared this information with them before. I decided I was going to go outside and have a cigarette–bad habit I know, still haven't been able to give it up. As I was sitting there, a feeling of electricity went through me and I heard a bird. I said out loud, "The time has come, I must prepare myself now."

After those words, my youngest daughter came running to the door and said, "I think Daddy is gone."

I did not run back into the house, because I knew in my heart of hearts that it was true, I knew the exact minute it happened. People often say two souls are connected; in this case they were right.

CHAPTER 4

THE FUNERAL

When I went back into the house, I just held my husband. Why couldn't I have waited to go outside? I really believe he planned it that way. He didn't want me there to see his last breath. I tried to close his eyes but I couldn't.

I called the hospice nurse; she was there in a matter of minutes. She called the funeral home and they came and took my husband away. I remember how sad it was; they made his bed and put a red rose on his pillow. The words we are sorry for your loss. It can't be true. There were so many feelings at that time; I don't know if it was relief, sorrow, sadness, disbelief or just plain emptiness. I am sure it was all of the above.

The first thing I did was have the hospital bed removed from the room. I just couldn't stand it. I wanted this all behind me. Then I removed all of his medications and everything that had to do with the illness. I thought if I could just get all of this out of my sight, it would be over. I didn't dare take time to think because I may fall apart, and I couldn't let that happen. I had too many things to do to prepare for the funeral. At this point, I was glad that I had made all of the arrangements ahead of time. I don't know how I would have made it through otherwise.

Our families came from all parts of New England. Church members, neighbors, friends and co-workers brought food for which I am thankful; therefore, I didn't have to think. It was just a flurry of activity.

When I walked into the funeral home on Friday and looked at my husband, I just couldn't believe it. He looked like himself again, no more sickness. His skin was no longer yellow. You couldn't tell that he had lost 40 pounds; I could no longer see his ribs. He actually looked like he had a grin on his face. He looked at peace.

We made it through all of the well wishers and "I am so sorry's." The day of his service, my daughter got up and said a few words about her father and then sang "The Lord's Prayer." To this day, I do not know how she made it through that song. She said she was singing for her daddy.

Hayward and Christine
May 11, 1997
Christine's Wedding Day

God blessed me with two beautiful daughters. My youngest daughter had written a poem for her father that was read during the service.

MY FATHER'S HANDS

by Tammy Tucker
My Father's hands can tell a story
of times of worry and times of glory.

My Father's hands are strong and true,
He held us together, He is the glue.

In His hands great memories cling,
in Judy, he did bring
and the winter, when he made ice,
in our back yard we skated, it was so nice.

My Father's hands on open arms,
Always kept us safe from harm.

Now we are in our darkest hour,
we turn to faith for saving power.

God's up in heaven, where we can't see,
may He lend His strength to thee.

If he should call you to His halls,
a great sadness would befall us all.

But to a thought, oh so grand,
One day in heaven, to hold
my Father's hands.

I Love You Daddy,

Love,
Tammy

left: Me, Tammy
and Hayward
1993
Tammy's Induction
into the Air Force

right: Tammy
and Hayward
1993
Tammy leaving
for Boot Camp

The pastor read a beautiful passage from Proverbs, and my brother, Robbie spoke.

Words spoken by my brother Robbie during the funeral service:

"During the days following his surgery, Hayward was struggling physically, emotionally and spiritually. And although this was a very difficult time for Hayward, he never lost his faith in God. Hayward and his daughter Christine kept a journal while he was in the hospital, and it was there where he penned this prayer."

EXCERPT FROM HIS JOURNAL

Lord,

I thank you for all the blessings you have laid upon me each and every day of my life. Today as everyday I rededicate my heart and soul to You the Almighty Father. I am but one of your servants and continually ask and require Your Guidance. Thank You Father. This disease, Father, is going to be my greatest challenge. Please help all those that love me get through this, and Lord, please help me. Spread Your Protective Light. Send knowledge, wisdom, patience and love through Thy Holy Spirit. We will be fighting this disease with the knowledge given from the Bible.

We laid him to rest with a military service. I thought that

it was owed to him since he served 20 years for his country. It was a beautiful ceremony, I just can't remember very much about it.

Family came back to the house afterwards. I was feeling very numb at this point. I remember thinking how can they laugh at a time like this; don't they know what just happened? How can anyone joke and be happy at a time like this? For the first time in my life I remember feeling very alone. I felt as if I had no connection with any of these people. Don't they realize what has just happened here? Don't they know that the love of my life is gone? I didn't know what to do or what to say. I can only remember feeling very numb. My daughters tried to reach out to me and comfort me. They needed it just as much as I did, but I honestly couldn't give them what they needed at the time. I was too busy and self absorbed to feel their pain; my pain was the only pain that mattered.

All of the family headed back to their homes the following day. My daughters stayed with me for another week, we could hardly even look at one another. None of us knew what to do with our pain. I certainly couldn't give any more. I had been too busy for the last two and a half months taking care of my husband. I was emotionally, physically, and spiritually drained at this point. I kept asking God why, why, why? The answers never came.

I kept feeling I was being punished. My daughters headed off to their own lives and families the following Saturday. I made them go home; I needed to wake up and be alone. I knew I had to face that first day with no one there. I thought I was ready for it. I needed to do it.

CHAPTER 5

ALONE

I remember, it was a Saturday and I made both of the girls go home. Tammy didn't want to go home because she was going to be so far away, Washington State, so she felt too disconnected from everything. Christine kept saying over and over again, Mom are you sure you don't want me to stay, I will be glad to stay with you longer. But I insisted that she go home, after all I needed to be alone. To think, to absorb all that had happened. It was something that I just felt that I needed at the time.

I remember when they both walked out the door, I wanted to scream, *please don't go, please don't leave me alone. I need you both; I can't bear the thought of being alone.* I couldn't get the words out. I was too stubborn, and after all, I was their mother. I needed to be strong for them. In the beginning I constantly tried to be so strong for everyone, never allowing myself to feel my pain.

I walked aimlessly through the house that day, sat on my porch, and stared into nothingness. What was I supposed to feel? What was I supposed to do? I had spent the last two and a half months caring for my husband. Where do I go from here? What kind of life could I possibly have now? For the first time, I felt like I had no purpose in life. Life just wasn't worth living anymore. I had lost my best and only friend. I just couldn't see past the pain. I began to grow very bitter towards everyone and everything. Nobody understood the kind of pain I was going through. No one had ever experienced it. I was the only one who mattered.

That night I slept with all the lights in the house on. I couldn't stand being alone. Fear, anxiety and all of the negative feelings had now set in. What kind of life is this? What kind of God are you? How can you let me experience so much pain? Why, why, why? My life is over. I have no future.

I had taken two and a half months leave of absence from work and a week off after I laid my husband to rest. It was now time to get on with life and put the past behind me. My employer was generally concerned for me, but I thought it was just pressure to get back to work. The fact was I had obligations, and they just wouldn't understand if I had to take more time off from work. So I returned that Monday.

I couldn't stand to see the pity on everybody's face that day. I couldn't stand to hear people say, "We're so sorry." I was sick of it! In my mind, they really didn't care. They were just saying the words. I hated words. It used to really anger me when people said, "I know how you feel." Unless you have experienced the death of a loved one, you don't know how I feel. You can say, "It must be very hard on you," or "It must be terrible." Just don't say, "I know how you feel," because you don't. Don't say, "I'm divorced, and it is the same kind of feeling," because it isn't. Divorce is a terrible thing too I understand, but your ex-spouse is still alive. When a spouse dies, they are no longer here. I am sure for all of those who said that to me, they definitely felt the daggers emanating from my eyes, but I didn't care because they didn't understand. They didn't know what kind of pain I carried.

I was a time bomb at this point. I got so sick with envy, listening to people say what they were going to do on the weekends with their families that I started disassociating myself with friends and family. I started living with my pain. It was my companion. I started building walls that no one could get through. I just couldn't deal with any more pain of any sort.

Easter was coming and that was my first holiday alone. My brother and his family and my daughter and her family came to spend it with me. I just went through the motions. We took the Easter lily that I had purchased through our church to the cemetery. I remember it was a beautiful day. The cemetery is a beautiful place with gazebos, water fountains, and beautiful flowers. My brother and his family wanted to have their picture taken in front of the little pond there. I tried relentlessly to get Christine and her family to have their picture taken there too, but she wouldn't hear of it.

I couldn't see her pain at this time. She was at the cemetery where her daddy was. Why on earth would she want to have her picture taken there? But I didn't see it that way then. I just thought she was being stubborn and obstinate. She never did have her picture taken that day. I can't say as I blame her. This was the beginning of the constant battles we were to face with each other.

She constantly tried to reach out to me in those days, but I just wouldn't have anything to do with it. I could get through this. I could do it alone. I had to be so strong for these last months and did it completely by myself; I didn't need anyone. She had so much pain. I know she needed me. I know she wanted me to put my arms around her and let her cry. I know she longed to be able to have me to turn to, so she could mourn her father. But my pain was the only pain that mattered. Please forgive me Christine.

I don't really know when it started, but soon I couldn't go through the night without having a glass of wine to relax me. A glass of wine to help me make it through the night, a glass of wine to take the loneliness away, a glass of wine to relieve my stress, a glass of wine because I had a bad day, a glass of wine because I had a good day, a glass of wine because it was good for your heart, a glass of wine for any reason at all. Soon the glass of wine turned into two glasses of wine, then three glasses. Then at 4:30, I couldn't wait to get home so I could have a glass of wine. This went on for six months. I couldn't make it through one single day without a glass of wine for whatever reason. After all, maybe I could numb the pain from being alone, and I knew I didn't have a drinking problem. Wine is good for you.

I don't know what made me realize that I was developing a problem, maybe the fact that I had to buy a 5 liter box of wine every week. I started buying the bottles, but it wasn't enough to last me through the week. So I went on to the boxes.

One particular evening after work when I was pouring my glass of wine, I realized I may be developing a problem, so I thought I'd just cut it down to one glass. I knew I was headed for disaster. The following Sunday when I went to church, I went up to the altar to pray. I knew I had to change my ways concerning drinking. Nothing else was wrong with me. I just needed to get used to the fact that I was now alone.

CHAPTER 6

FEAR

I know there are several different stages in the grieving process, and I honestly don't know which is supposed to come first, what exactly you are supposed to be feeling, or in what order. It seemed that mine were all jumbled up, and I couldn't tell from one day to the next where I was in this process. You can read all kinds of books and none of them will make sense to you.

Even today, at this point, I couldn't tell you exactly where I am in the grieving process. I just know that fear set in as soon as I accepted the fact that I was totally alone in the world.

I remember waking up one morning and said "Oh my God, how I am going to live? How will I pay my bills? I have no one to help me." Although my husband was in the military for 20 years, he thought he was immortal. You have two choices when you retire from the military, take full pension and it stops upon your death. Or take 50% of your pension and the surviving spouse is taken care of upon your death. We opted for the full pension. We had bills we had to pay and a mortgage. I remember the letter I received from the government upon his death: We are sorry for your loss; however, we will be deducting his retirement payment from your bank account—some gratitude for all of his years of dedicated service. I have filed a claim with the VA to fight for him. The doctors said his cancer was very rare, a derivative from his exposure to Agent Orange. I filed the claim 16 months ago, and I am still in the process of fighting it. I wrote my last statement of case in January. It is now July and there still has been no word.

As any blue collar married couple these days, we lived beyond our means–a mortgage payment, two vehicles to get us both to work, and the everyday living expenses, credit cards, etc. I am sure many of you can relate to that.

The reality is neither one of us attended college. There were no degrees; there were no high paying jobs, just everyday people trying to make ends meet. How in the world was I going to make it now? With the paycheck I receive I would probably only be able to pay my mortgage and car payment. I certainly wouldn't have enough money to even eat. I distinctly remember the conversation I had with my boss.

I think I am going to have to leave here. I don't make enough money here to support myself. What the heck am I supposed to do, sell my house? My health benefits were going to $360.00 a month and I just didn't make enough money to even be able to eat after that. She said, I understand. A little while later, she came back into my office and said maybe there was another way. Maybe, there was something else they could do. They gave me a car allowance to help me out. At this point I started blaming my husband and God for leaving me here to face all of this completely on my own.

How could you do this to me, what have I done so wrong in this world to constantly be punished like this? How will I be able to survive? How will I be able to support myself? Where are you when I need you? Why aren't you helping me? How could you allow this to happen to me? Why didn't you provide for me?

After my husband retired from the service, he really had a hard time adjusting to civilian life and he could never really find his niche. I was the strong one the one that always had a positive attitude. I always gave the pep talks. I really believed in him. He somehow, could never believe in himself. He always thought he would not amount to anything.

So in return, this is how I am rewarded. Now I started getting very angry with God and my husband, it was all their fault. I remember the day very clearly, it was Sunday, I couldn't go to church. I lay in bed all day, crying my heart out. Actually yelling at God, how could you do this to me? Why, why, why? Look at my life, look at everything I've done for everyone and no one is there for me. I was in so much pain. I didn't know where to turn or what to do.

About this time, the hospice social worker said there was going to be a support group for the bereaved. I just couldn't do that; I was too strong. I needed no one, but I finally talked myself into it. It was going to be held at a local church here in New Bern. I went, and I was the only one who showed up, another kick in the pants. Now they wouldn't be able to hold the group sessions. The Psychologist told me she would offer private sessions, but God knows I didn't have the money for that. So needless to say, I didn't go.

Everywhere I turned I ran into a brick wall. The social

worker would come and visit me every six weeks, but I put up a big front. I was all right. I was coping. I was carrying on. I just wanted her out of my house, so I could do this alone. I am a strong woman. I am the matriarch. I am the rock. I was the foundation of my so-called life.

My social worker told me I should start writing in a journal. I had several, but only picked it up once. I will share it with you. The only time I wrote in my Journal.

THOUGHTS FROM MY JOURNAL

June 22, 2003

All the books say you need to start a journal and put your feelings down on paper. It's hard to know where to begin. It's pretty sitting down here at the river. The water has always had such a calming effect on me. My whole life is in such turmoil right now. There are so many unknowns right now. What is to become of me, my life, and my relationship with Christine? It seems I'm always trying to fill a void that I just can't, always searching, always looking for you Honey, everywhere I go. I can't find you no matter how hard I look. Always the question of why, why, why? I went back to church today for the first time in over a month, still searching for unanswered questions. I even treated myself to going to the beach. I sat on the shore and watched children playing happily in the water. One woman sitting next to me told me she was being over protective because her son was outside. It brought Alec to my mind. I then took a walk on the beach and felt so alone. But all in all it felt really good to do something for myself for a change. I just wish you were here to share my day with. I miss your friendship, companionship and love. You always loved me no matter what. I know you must think it's an awful thing what is happening between me and Christine and it is. I don't know how to fix it anymore and I don't have the strength to even try. All my emotions are always right at the surface, and my feelings get hurt so easily. I expect her to understand and she can't. It hurts so much Honey. Losing you and now I'll probably lose her too. I went to her house the other day because she had surgery and it brought back those old feelings from you. I only stayed an hour because I felt so out of place. Angela was taking care of her and I felt like no one needed me anymore. My feelings are so raw. I am watching a young couple out on the river. It is very obvious they're happy and more than likely in love. I miss holding your hand. I miss cuddling up to you at night. I miss just knowing you'll keep me safe. There's an older couple feeding the ducks here at the river. It's amazing how much you notice when you have nothing but empty time. It is pretty here though.

For someone who didn't know where to begin I guess I've babbled on. One final note, I miss you and still love you. Wish you were here. Sounds like a post card. Next time I'll bring bread for the ducks and seagulls.
I Love You
XO XO

Hayward with our dog Mattie
September 2001
He loved his dog.

CHAPTER 7

IT'S MOTHER'S DAY

Here I am facing yet another holiday alone. My Mother, God Bless her, didn't want me to be alone for Mother's Day. My mother, 73 years old at the time, drove from Connecticut to North Carolina by herself, so I wouldn't have to be alone. I don't know of many mothers who would do that, but my mother did. My daughter and her family also came down. I didn't want to face Mother's Day. My husband wasn't here, and it was just another day I had to get through.

I was very angry at my daughter in those days and we couldn't say two words to one another without having a fight. They weren't there for long when we received a call from my son-in-law's mother saying she had broken down about 45 minutes from my house. It was about 90 degrees outside, and he had to go and pick her up and bring her back to my house. I was very angry, it was Mother's Day and I didn't want to share "my" day with anyone. When she arrived, I went outside and decided I was going to clean the pool and open it for the season. My mother came out to help me.

I just wanted everyone to get out of my house and leave me alone. If they didn't want to be with me to celebrate Mother's Day, then they could just go home. I was very selfish at this point. I couldn't wait for everyone to go home so my mother and I could go out to dinner, which is exactly what we did. My daughter's feelings were extremely hurt, but I didn't care. She was supposed to be there for me, and I shouldn't have to share it with her mother-in-law. So therefore, I didn't have to share a dinner with her. I didn't actually find out how hurt she was until later. But I couldn't see past myself in those days.

My mother spent about 10 days with me. During her stay she always loves to go and visit mobile home parks. We went, and I fell in love with a little mobile home. I did not purchase it at that time though. A couple days after my mother went home, I received a call from the mobile home park stating that if I went down right away and purchased a home I wouldn't have any payments until 2004. I thought this was a great idea. It was very hard on me going home night after night to the same house where my husband died. Every night it was a constant reminder of all that I had been through in the past couple of months.

If I had stopped for just one second, I would have realized it was not the time, but I went from one thing right to the next. I always had to be doing something so I wouldn't have time to think. If I stopped the reality of my husband's death would have been to real, and I couldn't allow that to happen. I stored his death in the back of my mind, because I was sick of dealing with it. I didn't want to feel the pain anymore. It had been two months, and I thought I should be starting to get better. The pain should start easing anytime now. So, I rushed right down there and put my deposit on my new house, picked out my land, and made arrangements with my realtor to sell my home. I have done everything in the last 16 months that they tell you that you shouldn't do. Don't do anything for the first year after your loss. Who were they? They didn't know anything.

I remember the day I brought my daughter to see my new lot. She was devastated, and she devastated me. She said, "Why mother, did you buy a lot here? I will have trouble selling it when you die." Her words cut through me like a knife.

I said to her, "How could you say such hurting words. Why can't you ever be proud of me?"

To her, my old home was safe; that is where her father was. It was because of her fears for me that the words escaped her mouth, but I didn't see it that way then. At that time it was just another hurt I had to experience. I wish we could have sat down and talked things through then, but it just wasn't meant to happen.

Buying that home was a major headache from the start. I would never do it again. When I originally bought it, the plans were to be completed in July in order for me to move right in. What a joke, it definitely did not happen that way. My home wasn't even put on my new lot until the end of August. The only reason it arrived then is because I called and threatened to obtain an attorney. So many promises they made then, and to this day, some of their promises have not been fulfilled. Now, my new modular is on the market.

I tried to get out of buying this home a month after I put my down payment on it, but they talked me out of it. I remember when the housing inspector came to my old house; there were so many things wrong with it. My cost was going to be $7000.00 to get everything fixed. I just panicked. When I called the mobile home place to state my concerns, they insisted I was doing the right thing, and besides, my new home was on their lot–not finished yet, but there nonetheless. I begged them to sell it to someone else, but it couldn't be done. So I proceeded with my plans.

I continually fought with them, the VA, and my daughter. Nowhere could I turn and have anything safe and comforting. Everywhere I turned it was another brick wall. I got so sick of everything.

Finally, my house had all the repairs completed, and it sold. My new home was finally ready to move in. It was September 27, 2003. They said I could move into the house before my closing date and before I closed on my old house. So I proceeded.

When I moved in, there was no electricity. The housing inspector wouldn't have it turned on because it didn't pass inspection for the sewer line and the decks. It had no hand rails and it would be a hazard for anyone if they fell. The health inspector came the following week, and they still wouldn't pass the inspection because there was going to eventually be raw sewage running into my backyard.

There was supposed to be top soil brought into my yard for the lawn, and that was never done either. Later, I was told it was because it cost too much money for the water tap. It was just one thing after another. The thing of it was, I trusted this young man and believed everything he told me. I am still very disappointed in him. When people would say, "All salespeople care about is your money," I never believed them. Unfortunately, it turned out to be the case in that instance. I would never recommend him to anyone now.

As a matter of fact, another couple that was there when I was buying my home came to my door a few months ago, and the lady was crying her heart out. It had been 10 months since she started the process, and to this day, they still aren't moved in.

So I guess I was pretty lucky that it only took 4 months for mine. I knew then, in my heart, that buying this home was a mistake, and since then, I am trying to listen to my instincts. I believe the feelings we have are from God. It is very hard to give up that control and let Him lead your life. "I surrender all" is a phrase of a hymn and is definitely something I am working on.

CHAPTER 8

IT'S FATHER'S DAY

Another holiday had just rolled around, only this one was his. My youngest daughter, Tammy, called me to see how I was coping. "Has Christine called you?"

"No," I said, feeling so hurt. "Why can't Christine call? Doesn't she care? She told me they would all be over. It's 4:00 P.M., and still I have not heard from my oldest daughter. I am going to go outside and mow the lawn. It is about 95 degrees outside, but I don't care. I have to do something, and she obviously doesn't care that I'm here and all alone. So what if it is her husband's first Father's Day. I am by myself."

They finally pulled up in my yard at 5:00 P.M. I didn't even turn the lawn mower off. They went in the house. I stayed outside; I was livid at this point. When I finally turned it off and went in the house with sweat pouring off of every part of my body, they were mad. I was mad. They wanted to know why I didn't turn off the lawn mower when they arrived. I wanted to know why she didn't call. We couldn't even talk to one another at this point.

Yelling and screaming our pain at one another, I said, "It's all about you, isn't it Christine?" She wanted to go to the cemetery. I had already been. With all of the pain and hurt in her eyes, trying to share her time with me, her husband, and her father-in-law, she turned around with tears in her eyes and left. I wanted to scream, *I'm sorry Honey; I didn't mean to hurt you.* I just couldn't get the words out. So instead, I sat down and wrote her a very hurtful letter, telling her everything she had done wrong.

In those days, Tammy was my savior; she is the only daughter who cared about me. She lives in Washington state, yet there wasn't a day that went by that she didn't call me to see if I was all right. Yet Christine lived 45 minutes away, and she couldn't bother.

Christine received my very nasty letter and called her sister, crying her heart out. I didn't care; she deserved it. She was never there for me. How ridiculous! I thought, as I later realized she had always been there for me. I just didn't see it. But at that time, I didn't care if I hurt her; she deserved it. She was the only one I could direct my anger at. I was not going to call her and apologize.

She called me. She wanted to come over and talk. I knew what I had done was wrong, but I couldn't apologize. She was the one who needed to apologize. When she arrived, I was mad at her. She didn't bring the baby. Lily, along with my other grandchildren, was the only thing that kept me going. So now even if we talked, I was going to be mad at her because once again she hurt me by not bringing Lily.

We talked, but they were just words. She cried, I cried, I tried to console her, but they were words that weren't really meant to heal. They were just words that I felt I had to say in order to rectify the situation.

Okay, so now we have apologized; it's time to get on with other things. The house, the house, the house, that is all that absorbed me during that time.

One day while I was driving, I was on the phone with Christine talking about how mad I was at the mobile home place. Bang! All of a sudden I became part of a car accident. By the way, it was not my fault. It was a young boy, eating a hot dog and drinking a soda, who decided he was going to turn into my lane. Great, another obstacle, Lord, when are you going to stop punishing me? What more can you do to me? Apparently, you don't think I've been through enough.

I want this to stop and stop now! How much more does He think I can take? I'm so sick of it all! But he gave me more. No matter what happened during that time, I continually prayed, mostly begging him for answers, asking for the pain to stop, why, why, why, over and over again. How many trials and tests do I have to complete before this is over? The pain just never eases; I feel like God must be very mad at me for some reason. What have I ever done that is so wrong in my lifetime? These questions continually go through my mind.

Chapter 9

The Big Move

I finally moved into my new home on September 27, 2003. I closed September 30, 2003. I was supposed to close on my house September 2, 2003 and twice more after that. That never came to pass. They always had a different reason why it couldn't be done. One of the dates was September 20, 2003. I remember that date; that is the day my sister Joanne died in 1980. That is also the day my daughter scheduled her Tupperware party, and she couldn't re-schedule it for me because she had re-scheduled it too many times before. Again, I felt this was just one more thing Christine found more important than me.

As it turned out, I wouldn't have been able to move that day anyway. Hurricane Isabel took care of that. Christine made me go to her house for the impending Hurricane, which I fought tooth and nail, but I did end up going.

I didn't have any major damage to my sold home. However, I lost all the trees in my yard. By the way, I think there were only two of us on the street that had that kind of damage. I remember looking at my yard and seeing devastation. How long is this going to go on? I didn't have a chainsaw. God knows I don't know how to use one anyway. I called Christine and explained what I had come home to. Once again, she dropped everything and said she would be right there.

I proceeded to go out into my yard and use a handsaw to start cutting down all the trees. As I was out there crying, asking God why again, I also prayed that he would send someone to help me. Why are you allowing all these things to happen to me Lord, when is it going to stop? Within the hour, not only did my daughter arrive, but one of the neighbors came over with a chain saw and cut down all the trees and removed all the debris from my yard.

I remember my daughter put Lily in her playpen and told me to sit and rest and they would take care of it. But I was angry; I should be out there helping. I felt useless. She was worried about me, but I didn't see it again. I didn't want to take care of the baby; I was embarrassed that I wasn't helping. I needed to make myself useful, but I sat out there with Lily in the heat. When all was complete, she made me go home with her. I was too tired to fight.

Upon my arrival home, all the trees that were carefully placed in my front yard to be taken away had been picked up. My next door neighbors had graciously removed them for me. I was truly thankful. I was so sick of facing all of this alone. I was beginning to feel very worn out. Between taking care of the house, the yard, packing, going to work, taking care of the car, paying the bills, dealing with the mobile home people, I was at the end of my rope. I wanted so much for my husband to be here with me. I wanted to share in my glorious new home. I wanted him to be proud of me. I wanted to feel his arms around me. I wanted to feel safe again. I missed him. I wanted him to hold me and tell me everything was going to be all right. How I longed for him! He would make all my pain go away, if I could just see him one more time. I love you, Honey.

I asked my daughter if she would come and help me move and stay with me so I didn't have to be in a new place all alone. Of course, she did. She did whatever I asked her to do; I just didn't see it then.

When moving day came, we were at odds again. It was my fault. She wanted to help, but because I was being the stubborn matriarch, I wanted to convey the message that I could do it alone. She was just here, so I wouldn't be alone. She would ask me over and over again what I wanted her to do. I didn't know, I couldn't even think of what I needed to do. But she carried on, going through the motions to make me happy. She is a tough little bird. She has a lot of her mother's traits. She never said a word. I wished she had, maybe I would have had a light bulb go off. But pain was all I could really see anyway.

She stayed for a couple of days, until I felt secure, then she went home. Home was now 4 hours away. In February my son-in-law's company was going to close, and he had accepted another position 4 hours north of me–one more punch, one more punishment. Now, I had no one here–no family, no friends, only those at work and they are really just friends at work. I had no one to talk to and nowhere to turn because I couldn't emotionally reach out to anyone. I couldn't allow myself to do that. I didn't want to talk about my husband's death anymore because it might make people uncomfortable.

People and friends say they will do this and that, but in reality, life goes on and soon your husband's or loved one's death is a past issue. Their lives go on, but yours stays the same. So then you think no one cares and no one understands, and you're right back where you started again.

Moving day came and went. It was closing day. After the closing, I came home to a flooded bathroom and hallway. The P trap under the sink had cracked, and there was water everywhere. Great, what else can go wrong? I called the mobile home people, and they came out and cleaned it up and got most of the water out of my rugs. Thank goodness that the storage area under my sink was complete with bath towels because every one of them was soaking wet. They helped stop some of the damage. I have no idea how long that leak was there because I didn't go into the back of the house.

I took a week off from work to get settled and then resumed my daily life again. I thought to myself at this point, *now you can begin a new life and have a new beginning.*

CHAPTER 10

WHAT NOW?

I had soon settled into my new home and was about to embark on my newfound life. I didn't have to go home and have the constant reminder of the absence of my husband by being in the same room where he had died. It was going to be a new beginning for me.

At first I thought this is great: I don't have to cook for anyone, clean when I want, eat what I want, don't have to get up and shower right away, shop only for myself. Me, me, me, it's all about me. How does one get used to being single when you have spent your lifetime with your soul mate? No one could compare to him.

You go through the motions everyday, always something missing, but you just can't pin point it. Then everyday turns out to be just like the day before. Why can't I fill that void? What is wrong with me? Why can't I ever be happy?

I watch a lot of *Lifetime* television, always watching about women survivors. One night an ad came on television about Internet dating. I thought, that's what I need, I need a companion, someone to take me out to dinner, talk to, etc. I was settled and now I had to do something else. I have always gotten through by doing, doing, doing. I can't have a lull because then the pain may come back, although it had never even come through yet.

So, I started dating Internet style. My first actual date was with someone in a wheelchair. I knew before I had actually met him that he was in a wheelchair. But I wasn't going to cancel the date because I was going to accept him for who is he was, and I didn't want to hurt his feelings. That is the honest to God truth to this day. The very next day, I told him it wasn't going to work because I wasn't ready, and I wasn't. He was a very nice man, and we had a great dinner together.

The next man I invited to my house, my daughters had a fit about. I don't blame them; it was a stupid thing to do. After meeting him I realized that he just wasn't going to work out. He hugged me, and I freaked out. It scared me to death. I remember I was up until 1:00 A.M. I wrote him an e-mail to explain to him that I just wasn't ready and the hug had scared me to death. I will never forget his response. He told me to drop dead and kiss his ass. I'm glad I escaped that one. The final one, also a very nice man, had just lost his wife that past September, so he was just beginning to experience all of the firsts. He had also made most of the decisions that I had.

It seems no matter what I do or where I look I can't find the right answer. I can't meet my husband, and that is what I am looking for. Although he was not perfect, no one adds up to him.

He loved me inside and out. He accepted me for all of my faults and shortcomings. In his eyes, I could do no wrong. I can't find him. I always push myself right to the limit. I don't allow myself to feel. I always have to move on to the next stage. If you take time for something, you may find out something you don't like. That is not a good place to be.

Loneliness and boredom had begun to set in. I didn't like this feeling. There was no one here for me, I was completely by myself and I didn't like it. I couldn't get out of it though. I had a house here and a job. This was my new life and I would just have to get used to it, because it couldn't change. So I told myself. I was lucky to have a brand new home and a job. I was luckier than others. This is just the hand that God chose to deal to me, so I just better get used to living this way.

The holidays were soon approaching–my first Thanksgiving and Christmas without my husband. Thanksgiving I could deal with, but Christmas, the time of giving and love and family and sharing and the whole world turns magical, I couldn't deal with that.

My parents and daughter came for Thanksgiving. It was a quiet day, and I was happy that my family was there. They talked about Hayward and how much he would love to eat. I tried to relate to their fond memories of him, but I wanted him here to share Thanksgiving.

We got through the holiday and I had to face Christmas. This time my parents wouldn't be here. My daughter and her in-laws would be here. I went into the bathroom to take a shower, and it all came crashing down. I wanted him here; I cried and cried my eyes out. I did not realize my daughter was in the bedroom and heard me. She wanted to know if I was all right. She wanted to help; she wanted her father too. I quickly stopped myself from crying and wished my husband a Merry Christmas.

I got through the day, trying to keep myself as busy as possible. I let them all go into the den to share their day, and I stayed in the kitchen. I didn't want to be part of their family. It was their family, not mine. They needed to share, and I was not part of them. Needless to say, I was very glad when the day ended. I wanted the holidays behind me. I didn't want to face the holidays without my husband. He loved the holidays. He embraced every magical moment in them. He was the rock of our family, and now we didn't have him. I couldn't go on like this. I couldn't go on without him. Please let the pain stop!

I took pictures of their family. I was satisfied not being a part of any of it. After all, I didn't belong anyway.

Chapter 11

The Turning Point

I had been going through the motions of life for the past 15 months. Going to work, cleaning the house, taking care of the yard and bills and resolved myself to think, this is just how it is going to be.

We were very short staffed at work, so I had been traveling from February to May to another office location, an hour drive each way until we replaced the person that left. I was tired and worn out, physically, emotionally and spiritually, but I continued on every day. Finally, we hired someone for the position and I was able to go to work at our corporate office 4 minutes from my home. I was tired, so tired. I had been working at that desk for about a month until we could get someone hired for the position here because that person transferred to another office. We were short staffed again.

It was Sunday, June 6, 2004 at 3:00 in the morning. I awoke in excruciating pain. I could hardly stand up. I thought I was going to pass out. I ran my wrists under cold water because I had always heard if you feel like you are going to pass out, run your wrists under cold water.

I got myself dressed and drove myself to the emergency room. I had no one else to turn to. I was the only one here. My daughter lived four hours away; I had no choice.

I spent three hours in the emergency room in terrible pain. I couldn't let them give me anything for the pain because I had no one to drive me home. They did an internal on me and I thought I would never make it through the pain. They said they couldn't find anything wrong so sent me home. I didn't show them the rash I had. The doctor told me to call my gynecologist as soon as possible the following week.

I called my doctor on Monday morning. On Monday afternoon I was admitted into the hospital. They still didn't know what was wrong. He also tried to give me an internal. It was just too painful. The pain was so horrible, they gave me morphine but it didn't even touch the pain. They performed every kind of test possible and everything came back normal. That doctor did see the rash but didn't really know if that was what was causing my pain. By my third day in the hospital, the rash had gotten worse, everywhere I scratched the rash, and my skin turned black and blue. The diagnosis was shingles. For anyone who has never had shingles, it is the most excruciating pain of all. I could barely walk, I was sick to my stomach for about 3 weeks and had constant diarrhea. The doctor told me to take consolation in the fact that I didn't get them on my face. I had them on my hip, backside, and leg. He put me on medication and said it would take 4–6 weeks for them to go away. He took me out of work for an indefinite amount of time.

I knew this was going to have consequences at work. Having shingles as it turned out has been the best thing that could have happened to me. When the doctor told me he was going to admit me, finally all of my fears came to the surface. It hit me like a ton of bricks. I was in a panic. Oh my God, I can't go to the hospital that is what happened to my husband. I am going to die. That's what happens when you go to the hospital. Oh no, I can't relive this. I just simply can't go through it again, but to the hospital I went.

The turning point was when I had just settled down into my hospital bed. Such a grieving came over me. I was completely alone. There was no family there, no daughters, no husband to console me, just blank empty ceilings that I continually looked up to. What a horrible feeling,

I had no one to hold my hand and say it's going to be all right. There were just the nurses trying to put the IV in my hand. I was so scared. All of a sudden I realized my husband was really gone and I was alone, truly alone. I couldn't do this anymore. I couldn't be alone. I didn't want to be alone. I was scared, life is too short. God, please help me! Please show me the way! Please direct my life; I am lonely Lord and afraid. I need my family; I want my family. I want to see my grandchildren grow. I want to be loved. I want to be surrounded by people who love me, people who make me feel like I belong, my family, the family that the Lord gave me, the family that loves me with all of my shortcomings and all of my faults, the family who I have dedicated my life to, the family who when they cry, I cry, when I cry, they cry, the family who has loved me and always believed in me throughout this past year and a half and who never turned their backs on me no matter what I did, the family who I cannot go on without another day.

At that point, I realized that no job or house can ever

compare to your family and the love that God has put there for you to share and rejoice in. We need to love one another and be grateful for this great gift of life that is meant to be shared.

CHAPTER 12

THE FINAL DECISION

I was out of work for three weeks. During my stay at home, I started having dreams about my husband for the first time since he died. One night, I dreamed I was upstairs in a house, looking out the window, and he was there on the ground. He told me he was going to help me move. All of my belongings were in the back of a trailer. He turned and walked away. I believe he was there with my message; *it is time to move on.* As I watched him walk down the road, he looked very sad. I don't know if it was because of me or if he was trying to say goodbye.

In another dream he was with me going over a bridge. It's hard to figure out what your dreams mean, but I believe it meant that it has been a very long bridge from pain to the realization of what is important in life.

My daughter came down to be with me while I was in the hospital, and then she came to the house to care for me when I got home. She has always been there for me all along. I was just too blind and stubborn to see it. Tammy only calls once a week now. She went to school to become a medical assistant. I am very proud of her; she did this while trying to raise three young children. Tammy has always done things the hard way. She is very much like her father. I am very proud of both of my daughters. We have come a long way since March 26, 2003.

Christine was a music teacher and gave up her profession when she had her first child. She wants to stay home and raise her daughter. They are thinking of having another child soon. I want to be there to share that with both of my daughters. I want my grandchildren to know who their grandfather was and what he was all about, and I will teach them that.

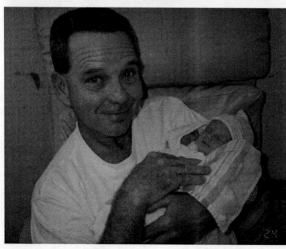

above: Alec, Jacob, Grampie and Kierah July 2001 We went out to Washington State to visit our daughter and her family.

left: Grampie and newborn Lily August 24, 2002

Grampie and Lily
March 2003
Grampie talking on the phone to Tammy. He was in a lot of pain
but loved his grandchildren and always put them first.

I called my realtor and put my house up for sale. I went to work and told my boss what my plans were. I don't think they are very happy with me right now. They have taken away all of my responsibilities at work. At first I felt like I was once again being punished for being sick and out of work. The day I returned she told me it had been like being on roller coaster ride with me this past year, and I can honestly say it has. I pray that she will never experience the pain and suffering I have experienced this last year. She said she didn't want me to have any stress. She said I hadn't dealt with the fact that my husband died. Up until this point, I hadn't dealt with my husband's death. To a point she is correct, but until you have walked in the shoes that I have walked in this past year, there is just no way of knowing what kind of pain and anguish I have been through.

For these words spoken by my boss I am truly thankful, it woke me up. I guess I needed someone to actually say the words. Three days later I sat down at my computer and started putting all my feelings to words. As a result, you are now reading "The Journey." I wish I didn't have to write this book because now unfortunately my husband's death is real, and I have finally come to the realization that I have lost my one true love.

My husband was and still is my best friend, and there isn't a day that goes that I don't miss him. I believe I will miss him until the day I die. He has left a hole in my heart that right now just cannot be filled. I have come to acceptance. I believe acceptance means your heart and mind tell you he is gone. What we do from that point on is totally and completely up to us.

My mind has accepted the fact that he is gone, but my heart is still having a hard time with it. What happens from this point forward I cannot tell you. I still don't know what the future is going to bring, and it is scary. I am selling my home, moving to a new area, but the most important thing of all is that I am going to take a couple of months off and spend time with my family, the family who I have put off for 16 months now. I am going to go out to Washington state and spend time with my daughter, son-in-law, and my three grandchildren.

No one can tell you what you are supposed to be feeling. Everyone grieves in a different manner. Lord, I wish there were a manual on it, but there just isn't. Grieving is a very personal thing, and only you can work through it. It takes time, and some people take longer than others. Time does heal, but it's a process.

Some people can embrace their pain like I did, but most important of all is to embrace your family and all who love you. They are truly the gifts from God and He will never let you down. Unfortunately, it took me a long time to see that, but he has been by my side every step of the way. If it weren't for my faith, I never would have made it through.

I wish at this time to thank my daughters, my family, friends, co-workers and employer. I thank God everyday that he has blessed me with all of you. The healing process begins with acceptance, and I don't believe it will last as long as getting to this point in my life.

I pray for all of you who may possibly be experiencing the same thing I did. Just know that everything you are going through is completely normal. The journey to get there can sometimes be rough. When you do finally reach your final destination, the trip will be worth it.

I have recently hung a saying that someone gave me a few years back on my bathroom mirror to make sure I read it every day. It has hung meaninglessly on my refrigerator for the past few years. It has new meaning now. I hope it will help you also.

We may not like the present circumstances in our life
and as a result try to resist them
but most likely we are experiencing exactly what we need

in order to grow spiritually
nothing happens by chance or accident
when we learn to be grateful for things just as they are
greater good will flow to us
adopting an attitude of nonresistant patience
at the same time praising everything and everyone in our life
is the key to joyful living.

The past will always be with me as well as the many mistakes I have made, but now I can honestly say I am looking forward to what the future holds. My faith in the Lord will sustain me.

Hayward and me
March 2003
Walking the halls of the hospital was indeed a very hard
task for Hayward; he tried to be so brave for us. His
strength and endurance I will always remember.

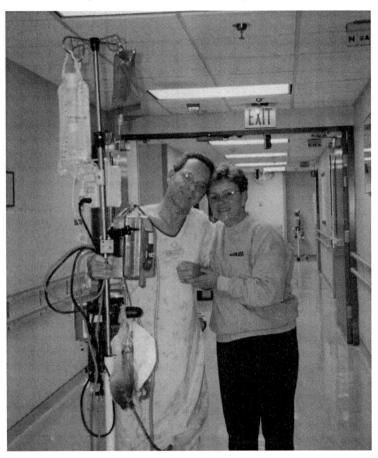

Until we meet again, My Love
In loving memory of my husband
Hayward George Rogers, Jr.
June 29, 1950 - March 26, 2003

Contact Sandy Rogers
or order more copies of this book at

TATE PUBLISHING, LLC

127 East Trade Center Terrace
Mustang, Oklahoma 73064

(888) 361 - 9473

Tate Publishing, LLC

www.tatepublishing.com